有時
A Time

祂使萬事各按其時變得美好。
He has made everything beautiful in its time.
（傳道書 當代譯本 Ecclesiastes 3:11）

徐仰聖
Frank Chui

有時
A TIME

作者、詩作改版、翻譯、攝影、美術設計：徐仰聖
Author, Poetry Converter, Translator, Photographer, Art Designer: Frank Chui

出版者：華品文創出版股份有限公司
台北市中正區重慶南路一段57號13樓之1
電話：02-23317103
Publisher: Chinese Creation Publishng Co., Ltd.
13F.-1, No. 57, Sec. 1, Chongqing S. Rd., Zhongzheng Dist., Taipei City 10045, Taiwan (R.O.C.)
Tel: +866-2-2331-7103
E-mail: service.ccpc@msa.hinet.net.net

版次：2025年3月初版
Edition: First edition, March 2025

定價：新台幣300元
Price: NT$ 300

國際書號：978-626-7614-07-5
ISBN: 978-626-7614-07-5

本書言論、圖片文責歸屬 作者所有
Copyright © 2025 Frank Chui

版權所有 翻印必究
All Rights Reserved.

除非另有說明，經文均引自《和合本2010（和合本修訂版）》，版權屬香港聖經公會所有，蒙允准使用。
凡註以「新譯本」的經文均引自《聖經新譯本》，版權屬環球聖經公會所有，蒙允准使用。
凡註以「當代譯本」的經文均引自《聖經-當代譯本》，版權屬國際聖經協會所有，蒙允准使用。

All Scripture quotations, unless otherwise indicated, are taken from the Holy Bible, New International Version®, NIV®. Copyright ©1973, 1978, 1984, 2011 by Biblica, Inc.™ Used by permission of Zondervan. All rights reserved worldwide. www.zondervan.comThe "NIV" and "New International Version" are trademarks registered in the United States Patent and Trademark Office by Biblica, Inc.™

Scripture quotations marked ESV are from the ESV® Bible (The Holy Bible, English Standard Version@), copyright© 2001 by Crossway Bibles, a publishing ministry of Good News Publishers. Used by permission. All rights reserved.

Scripture quotations marked KJV are from King James Version. Public domain.

獻給你和我：
為了「安」與「樂」，
我們在生活中苦戰良久。

To you and me,
we have been die fighting
for peace and joy for so long.

黃序

　　認識徐仰聖和李淑蘭已經有二十年，在印象中，他們都是很有才華的人。當年我在福音戒毒機構擔任主席的時候，淑蘭利用她長袖善舞的能力，在籌款上給了機構很大的幫助；仰聖的才華更是多方面的，我過去認識的他，在武術和平面設計方面有傑出不凡的能力，想不到他在詩詞歌賦和攝影方面的恩賜更加出類拔萃！尤其令我佩服的，是他把信仰應用於生活的得心應手與隨意沾來。

　　不過，仰聖的作品令我感動的，並非單單從詩意的文字和美麗的相片而來，它令我想起我的弟兄在這二十年來的掙扎與改變……我在仰聖和淑蘭的婚禮中曾經給他們訓勉，其後看着他們倆人行過死蔭幽谷的日子，也看到他們之間緊籮着手不放的愛情是何等感人！難以忘記當日在機場送別他們移民美國的那一刻和那一次禱告，更想不到當日的祝福後面充滿上帝的印證，看到仰聖這些年間的生命蛻變，怎能不感恩！上帝的恩典一直追隨着他們的家庭。

　　傳道書是智者對人生的反省，其中膾炙人口的一段是這樣的：「凡事都有定期，天下每一事務都有定時。生有時，死有時；栽種有時，拔出有時……哭有時，笑有時；哀慟有時，跳舞有時……上帝造萬物，各按其時成為美好……」這本詩集也是一個對人生認真的人真誠的反省和分享，同樣是一段平凡又不平凡的人生軌跡之見證：凡事都有定期，一個願意敬畏上帝的人無論經過怎樣的高低起伏，他的人生仍然是福杯滿溢，到了結果的時候，就豐收纍纍。

黃永輝
基督教巴拿巴愛心服務團主席 (1993~2013)
香港循道衛理聯合教會香港堂義務教士

Foreword by Wong

  It has been twenty years since knowing Frank and Helen, both are so gifted. When I was the chairman of an evangelical drug rehabilitation institution, Helen managed to give huge support on fundraising for the organization with her remarkable interpersonal skills. On the other hand, Frank's talents are multifaceted, he particularly has distinguished abilities in martial arts and graphic design. Yet, I never knew that his talents in poetry writing and photography are so exceptional, particularly regarding his application of faith to life in such a natural way.

  However, the most touching part of this book does not come from his poetic writing nor the beautiful photographs, but from it reminding me of his struggles and transformation throughout the past twenty years… I could still remember the scene when I gave the admonishment speech in the wedding of Frank and Helen, and later, the days when they walked through the valley of the shadow of death, witnessing how moving their tenacious love was! I also find it hard to forget that moment when bidding them farewell and praying for them for their emigration at the airport. How could I imagine that the blessing given on that day would be so fully confirmed by God? When looking back at Frank's transformation throughout these years, how could I not be grateful? God's grace has always been chasing so earnestly after their family!

The book of Ecclesiastes is a reflection of life of the wise, including the following very popular passage, "To every thing there is a season, and a time to every purpose under the heaven: A time to be born, and a time to die; a time to plant, and a time to pluck up… A time to weep, and a time to laugh; a time to mourn, and a time to dance… He hath made everything beautiful in his time…" This poetry anthology is also a sincere reflection of life and the sharing from a person who takes life seriously, a testimony of an ordinary yet extraordinary trajectory of life as well. To everything there is a season! No matter what ups and downs a person who is willing to fear God has been through, his life still overflows with blessings. When it comes to the time to bear fruits, there will be a plentiful harvest!

— Samuel Wong

Chairman, The Barnabas Charitable Service Association Ltd, Hong Kong (1993~2013)
Local preacher, Chinese Methodist Church, Hong Kong

劉序

  在教會裏認識徐仰聖弟兄時，只知道他是個不苟言笑的習武之人（詠春拳教學並進），後來在服事中有了更多的接觸，漸漸和仰聖與他的妻子淑蘭近距離的熟識了。在我們這個瞬息萬變的時代，很難想像一個人能夠兼顧兩種截然不同的領域：武術的嚴格紀律和詩歌的自由抒情。然而，仰聖弟兄做到了。近年來他又醉心於攝影，以其獨到的眼光捕捉生活中的雲那。於是心中的執念，隨興的詩句，和流光彩影的結合，誕生了這本集子。

  仰聖的詩洋溢着真摯的情感和深刻的思考，是他對信仰、人生和自然的獨特體悟。他的照片則是身邊的歲月靜好時光不老，處處顯出神創造的驚喜，這是他對生命的熱愛和追求。

  想想，武術和詩這兩者看似毫不相干，但在仰聖身上並不違和。在武術的訓練中，他磨練了意志，鍛煉了體魄；在詩句的創作中，他抒發了情懷，開闊了思維，且行且珍惜，至終使他做了真正的自己。作為基督徒，生命可以是豐富多彩的。我們不必拘泥於傳統的思想模式，而可以勇敢地探索未知的領域。只要我們心存真誠，以神的教導為指引，我們就能夠在人生的道路上走得更遠、更好。

我相信，這本集子一定會帶給讀者們美的共鳴和休閒中的享受。

在此，向仰聖弟兄表示衷心的祝福，也希望這本集子獲得讀者們的喜愛。

劉西傳道暨劉王邦聰師母

洛杉磯靈糧教會

Foreword by Liu

When I met Brother Frank in church, I only knew that he was a reserved martial arts practitioner (going in teaching and studying Wing Chun Gung Fu). While later having more contact with him through serving in church, we gradually got to know Frank and his wife - Helen better and we felt close as family. In such an ever changing era, it is hard to imagine a person can manage two totally distinct domains: the highly self-disciplined demanding martial arts and the liberally lyrical poetry, but Brother Frank did it. In recent years, he enjoys photography, using his one of a kind perspective to capture moments after his footprints. Therefore, with the determination in heart, the spontaneous lines of poems, along with the mesmerizing images dancing in the light, give birth to this anthology.

Frank's poetry overflows with honest emotions and deep thinking, which is his unique understanding in faith, life and nature. The surrounding serenity moments that are captured through his lens displays endless surprises in God's creations, and they seem never to grow old. Such is his passion and pursuit in truth.

Think about this, martial arts and poetry are not to be relevant, but in Frank they achieved harmony. In martial arts training, he sharpens his will, strengthening his physique; in the creation of poetry, he expresses his feelings, broadens his mind, treasuring every moment life has to offer, he finally finds his true self. In a Christian world, Frank has been blessed abundantly. We don't need to be constrained by the traditional model of thinking, but dare to explore the area of the unknown. Only when we bear sincerity in heart, holding God's teaching as our guidance, then we shall walk steadily and better moving forward in life.

Hereat, I express my cordial congratulations to Brother Frank. I hope this anthology brings aesthetics and enjoyment to the readers while leisurely sharing the fruit of his effort.

Wishing this anthology be favored by all readers.

— Charles Liu and Joyce Liu
Minister and wife, Bread of Life Church

自序

《押韻的詩句》

平仄去入賦抑揚，

獨句語寡意難張，

行文對偶道更詳，

押韻無曲也繞樑。

　　押韻是趣味盎然的。不是嗎？押韻的字句，配以旋律成為歌曲，就能輕而易舉的在人們心裏留痕。熱話交談，偶有兩句說話押韻，即成為笑點，催旺氣氛。無論在中文或是英文的文學世界裏，押韻都有着歷史悠久的所屬專區：教孩童們嘴忙若飴的童謠，讓成年人怦然回甘的詩詞。好些這等過百年的陳飴舊酒，仍不時成為編輯或設計師的桌面新案，或出版社再版的不日出品。

　　有趣的是，好些越是近代的詩作，中文的也好、英文的也好，押韻被悄然的廢去了尊貴的位份。那麼，這又有什麼樂趣呢？

　　筆者在二千年代後期開始寫詩，至今寫的都是中國古詩體五七言絕律詩。這種體裁的特色是每首詩的詩句數量是四或四的倍數，一首詩可以是句句押韻或者好些詩句押韻，而每行詩句則固定由五個字或七個字組成。最大原因讓筆者堅持這種格式的是它的工整規格：是個局限，也是個挑戰；自從寫成了頭一、兩首以後，就有了往績來抱持「早晚完成這一首」的心態來寫接下來的每一首；當中那保證的多巴胺，在過程中燃燒澎湃的寫作動力，在竣工時回饋莫大的獎賞。

筆者的詩作，秉持某些原則：國、粵語押韻，用字能與當代讀者溝通，而且要有相片來強化意境。早期的詩作語調較為晦暗，不少在訴說着人生的無奈；後來受到劉西傳道的提點才「提高」了作品的「亮度」，多了一點光明。

這一本詩集由四大元素所組成：

一、詩：中文的詩固然是最基要的部分，而這些詩的英文版卻是中文版的轉換（並非直白的翻譯）；每一句仍然保留中文版的主要意思，但詞類的舖陳卻是重新處理，好使押韻（讓我們保留這份樂趣吧！）。（這好比一齣電影，原本製作自某城或某國，後來給翻拍成另外一個地方的版本，兩個版本的細節不盡一樣，但故事和劇情大致相同。）

二、相片：本書所採用的相片，全為筆者生活的影像記錄，親自攝影，不假外求；用在書中的，部分給作出了裁切，全部沒有後期加工。

三、短文：筆者以一、兩句說話來延伸或加強每首詩的重點。

四、《聖經》的經文：撇除宗教背景，《聖經》一直被視為至高的經典。（坊間不少書籍以《 __ __ 聖經》來命名以表示該著作在其知識領域上的權威。）對於基督徒來說（包括筆者），《聖經》是一本生活指南，是叫人活得更豐盛的一本著作。有見及此，筆者從《聖經》中引用一至兩句經文來回應每首詩的主旨，也希望帶來啟發。

以上的四項結集而成的這書，希望能為您在生活裏多開一扇窗，為您在路途上再添一點光。

祝福閣下！

Preface

Rhyming Lines

Level, Oblique, Going and Checked,
intonation's born when tones connect.
Not many a word in a sentence set,
barely could the meaning be expressed.
Lines in pairs mark a track,
leading into more details ahead.
Rhyme need not have a melody attached,
it resounds as good as it gets.

    Rhyming is fun, isn't it? Rhyming wordings cooperating with melody creates a song that can effortlessly mark in the hearts of people. In the midst of a conversation, occasionally having two sentences that rhyme would turn the moment into a point of laughter, adding warmth to the atmosphere. Whether in the Chinese or English literature world, rhyme has its own specific sector with a long history: nursery rhymes like candies that keep children's mouths busy, and poetries that throb the hearts of adults in an aftertaste. Many of these over-hundred-year well-aged candies and wines, still become new projects for editors or designers from time to time, or to be reprinted by publishers as products coming soon.

Interestingly, quite some of the more modern poetries, whether it is in Chinese or English, rhyme has quietly been revoked its noble status. Well, then, what fun is it?
I started writing poetry in the late 2000s, and what I have written so far has always been in an ancient Chinese poetry format called "Five, Seven Words Rhyming Poem". Such a format has the characteristics that each poem composed in four or the multiple of four lines, all rhyme or some rhyme with either five or seven characters in each line throughout the work. The biggest reason for me to stick to this format is its neatness, it is a limitation but also a challenge. Ever since I achieved the first one or two pieces, I hold fast to my track record with the mentality of "I will finish this one sooner or later" whenever I work on a new piece. It comes with a guaranteed supply of dopamine which ignites the surging motivation for writing during the process, and as a grant reward upon completion.

My poems adhere to certain principles: rhyme in both Mandarin and Cantonese, wordings communicative with contemporary readers, and match with photos to enhance the conception. The tone of my early works was relatively gloomy. Many of them spoke of the helplessness of life. Later, under the admonishment of Minister Charles Liu, the brightness of my works was tuned up.

    This anthology of my poems consists of four major elements:

1. Poetry: The Chinese poems are no doubt the fundamental part. While the English version of these poems are the conversion of their Chinese counterparts (instead of their literal translation) in which each line of them retains the main idea from the Chinese version still, the presentation order of the parts of speech was handled independently in order to rhyme (let's keep the fun, shall we?). (Like a movie originally produced in a country or city, but later was filmed into another area's version. The details between the two versions are different, but the storyline and the plot are very much the same.)

2. Photos: The photos used in this book are all my visual records of life, none was taken from outside sources. Some of the photos featured are cropped, but none of any of them have been touched up by any other means.

3. Short essay: One or a few sentences to extend or reinforce my communication through each poem.

4. Bible scriptures: Regardless of religious background, the Bible has always been deemed as a supreme classic. (Many books in the market titled "_____ Bible" to suggest its authority in its discipline) To Christians (including me), it is a directory of life, a book that

can guide a human being to live more abundantly. In such a sense, I cited a verse or two from the Bible for each poem in response to its subject matter and wish to bring forth some inspiration.

This book, compiled from the above four elements, hope to open you up another window in your life, or light your path up a little more for your journey ahead.

Blessings!

目錄　　　　　　　　　　　　　　　　　　　　　　　　CONTENTS

黃序	01 / 03	Foreword by Wong
劉序	05 / 07	Foreword by Liu
自序	09 / 12	Preface
有詩有時	20 / 19	A Time to Rhyme
雨後	22 / 21	After the Rain
春雪	24 / 23	Spring Snow
華冕	26 / 25	Crown of Beauty
心水	27	Water in the Mind
虹心	30 / 29	Heart of the Rainbow
煙虹	32 / 31	Rainbow in the Steam
花樣人間 I	34 / 33	Flowery World I
花樣人間 II	36 / 35	Flowery World II
花樣人間 III	38 / 37	Flowery World III
花樣人間 IV	40 / 39	Flowery World IV
花非花	42 / 41	Flowers, not Flowers

那樹	**44 / 43**	The Tree
紫妝	**46 / 45**	Violet Makeup
友風花	**48 / 47**	Befriend Wind and Flowers
人言可貴	**49 / 50**	Precious Words
花勝昨	**52 / 51**	Sweeter than Yesterday
緩色退	**54 / 53**	Slow the Fading Down
平安	**56 / 55**	Peace
未通神	**57 / 58**	Can't Trade with God
朝花夕拾	**60 / 59**	Gather the Warmth
風雨復晴	**61 / 62**	A Clear Sky Restored
重生	**64 / 63**	Born Again
一天	**65 / 66**	One Sky, One Day
謝詞	**67 / 70**	Acknowledgements

A Time to Rhyme

Gale scrolls the sea
do whitecaps heap,
Pounding up and down
as if heartbeat,
Left not sit speechless
by the recurrent never cease,
But enjoy a time to rhyme
from all the ups you reap.

起與落，兩者都來而又去、去又復還，兩者都試圖令你印象難忘。
他們哪一個令你歡喜？哪一個值得你留住呢？

Ups and downs, both keep coming and going, both want to impress you in some ways.
Which one do you care for? Which one is worth to stay?

「哭泣有時，歡笑有時。」

"A time to weep, and a time to laugh."

(傳道書 當代譯本 *Ecclesiastes* KJV 3:4)

【有詩有時】
風臨翻海白浪至,
匉訇起落心率似,
莫坐無言事無止,
且醉有詩在有時。

※ 匉訇：國、粵語按其發音與「砰（烹）轟」同，形容大聲。

After the Rain

Melancholy drawn by the sky of grey,
The gloomy clouds for whose attention to pay?
Downpour and thunder did make their way,
Frost up a pillow that keeps you to stay up late.
No more rain the next day,
yet the gloom didn't go away.
Grateful still is the meadow's willing to stay,
With the red leaves,
they weaved a new look for praise.
Stunning in the new rainy coats are they,
which are dearly heavenly-made.

一定會有為你守候、為你打氣的，甚至不畏艱難與你共同進退的人。

There must be someone who would stand by you, cheer you up, and even advance and retreat with you regardless of the hardships.

【雨後】

灰天黯然惹惆悵，
烏雲無彩誰瞻仰？
夜雨滂沱雷聲響，
難眠枕上再加霜；
翌晨雨過天依樣，
猶幸綠茵未揚長，
更承紅葉賣新相，
載水照天煥靈窗。

「（神）賜給他們華冠代替灰塵」

"(God) bestow on them a crown of beauty instead of ashes."

(以賽亞書 新譯本 Isaiah 61:3)

※ 煥靈窗：使靈魂之窗煥發。

Spring Snow

Early spring but lack of chill.
Green leaves thrive
yet winter still.
Who blew the snow
across the northern sill?
But the moonly hue
is more charming
in Bradford filled.

在一個不下雪地區的春天看到雪,看起來不太對勁。
但事實上,這只是「看起來」而已。

Seeing snow in spring in a region that does not snow seems not right.
But the fact is, it only "seems".

「『因我自己知道我為你們所定的計劃,是使你們得平安,而不是遭受災禍的計劃;要賜給你們美好的前程和盼望。』這是主的宣告。」

" 'For I know the plans I have for you,' declares the Lord, 'plans to prosper you and not to harm you , plans to give you hope and a future.' "

(耶利米書 新譯本 Jeremiah NIV 29:11)

【春雪】
早春伊始寒意缺,
綠葉雖榮冬未絕,
誰敢北門暗吹雪?
原來豆梨色賽月。

※ 豆梨的花期在春天。

Crown of Beauty

Spring rain
does prosper all things.
But I, frosty crowned
a hoary bearing.
Scoff not by saying,
"white-haired no better than
the fresh and sprouting".
A good old scene can be
unparalleled and fascinating.

【華冕】
春雨送來萬物興，
唯我暮顏霜滿頂，
莫笑白首遜新青，
蒼華也有絕風景。

有一種偏頗叫「比較」，
它不是叫你看到自己的不足，而是不讓你看見自己的好處。

There is a kind of bias called "comparison".
It does not make you see your shortcomings but keeps your eyes off from your strengths.

「你的日子如何，你的力量也必如何。」

" Your strength will equal your days."

（申命記 Deuteronomy 33:25）

Water in the Mind

Still water mirrors
thousands of matters,
A calm mind
can hold a piece of sky.
Wind and rain
make ripples bolder,
Still unchanged
is the Kingdom
in the most high.

【心水】
止水如鏡映萬千,
心平能載一片天,
風吹雨灑生華漣,
上天如何未改變。

也許之前的「天公不作美」是為了後來的驚喜作準備。

Perhaps the previous weather was not cooperating was a preparation for a surprise.

「你們要稱謝天上的 神，因為祂的慈愛永遠長存。」

"Give thanks to the God of heaven. His love endures forever."

(詩篇 Psalms 136:26)

※雨天過後地上積水的倒影（在本頁和上一頁的所有圖片）
Reflection on puddles after a rainy day (images on this page and the previous page)

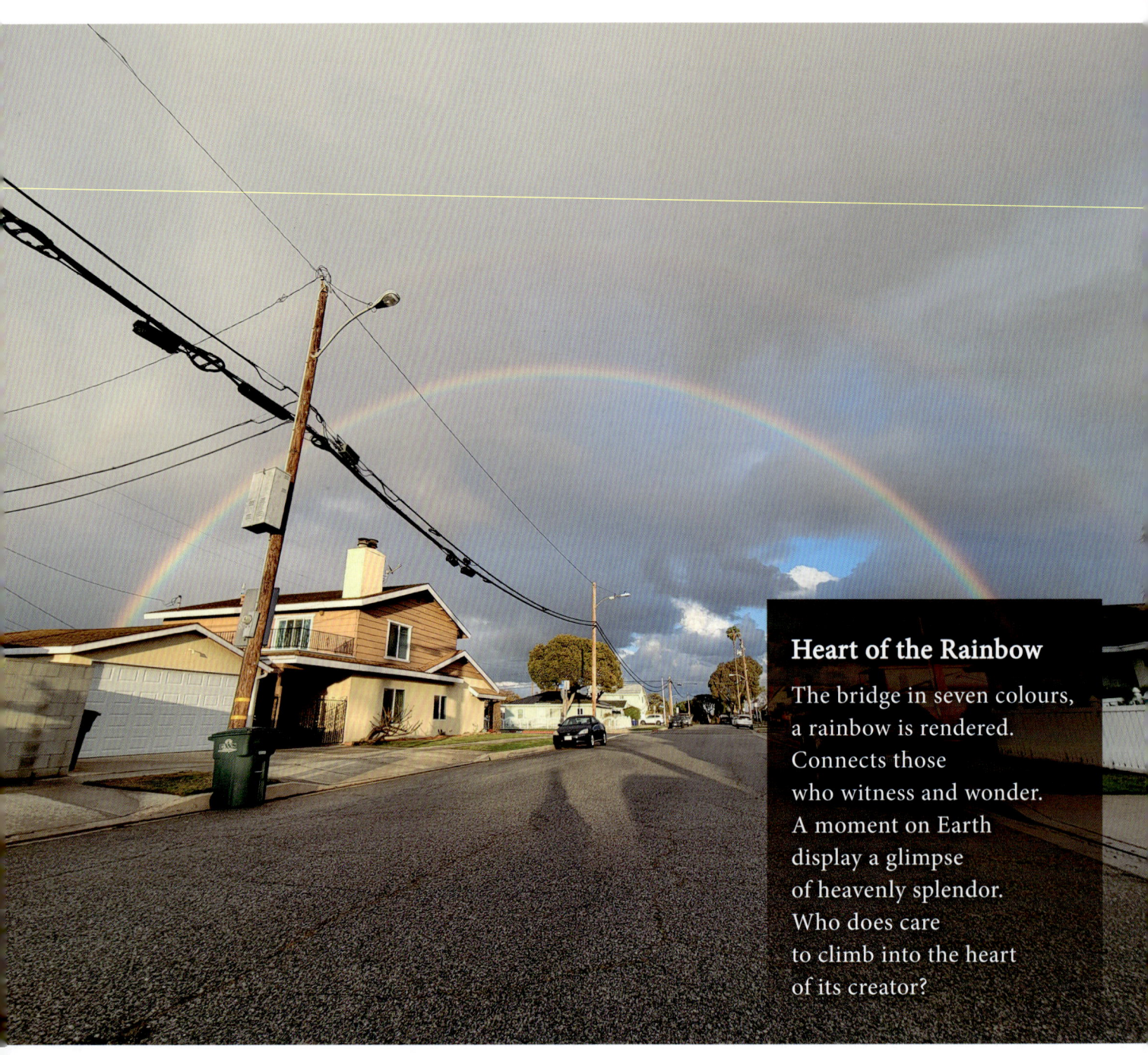

Heart of the Rainbow

The bridge in seven colours,
a rainbow is rendered.
Connects those
who witness and wonder.
A moment on Earth
display a glimpse
of heavenly splendor.
Who does care
to climb into the heart
of its creator?

【虹心】
彩橋一度虹一彎,
相連同睹同讚嘆,
天榮一剎耀塵凡,
可往造者心裏攀?

保持抬頭挺胸,才能有遼闊的視野,也不會錯過彩虹。

Keep your head up and your shoulders back so that you can have a broad view and never miss the rainbow.

「當我(神)看見彩虹在雲中出現的時候,就會記得我與地上一切生靈立的永約。」

"Whenever the rainbow appears in the clouds, I (God) will see it and remember the everlasting covenant between God and all living creatures of every kind on the earth."

(創世記 當代譯本 Genesis 9:16)

Rainbow in the Steam

Good old bench
well beaten by storm.
Steaming when again
meeting the noonday warmth.
Intrigued to squat
for the vision came along.
Thrilled to see a rainbow
there lowly dawn.

美事也會臨到卑微之處。
Beautiful things
still come to the lowly.

【煙虹】
飽嚐雨打老木櫈，
再遇午陽白煙騰，
妙象奪神誘蹲身，
低處喜見虹來問。

「祂從灰塵裏抬舉貧寒的人，
　從糞堆中提拔貧窮的人。」
"He raises the poor
from the dust
and lifts the needy
from the ash heap."
(*詩篇* 新譯本 Psalm 113:7)

【花樣人間 I】

樹上花、路緣花，
誰根不從爛泥巴？
哪朵能逃風雨打？
誰予傲氣由矜誇？

種子不能選擇土壤，人們也不能安排際遇。

Seeds cannot choose the soil, and people cannot arrange their encounters.

「使你與人不同的是誰呢？
你所有的有哪一個不是領受的呢？」

"For who makes you different from anyone else?
What do you have that you did not receive?"

(歌林多前書 1 Corinthians 4:7)

Flowery World I

Flowers in the trees,
flowers by the curb.
Whose root is not
from the messy dirt?
Which is proof
from the storm to hurt?
Who due the praise
and pride to serve?

Flowery World II

Flowers behind ears,
flowers beneath soles.
Bloom or broken,
one step to go.
Whose fate is better?
Who knows?
Neither is higher
and neither is low.

花的美在於色澤，人的美在於品格。

The beauty of flowers lies in their colours,
while the beauty of people lies in their character.

「魅力是虛假的，美貌是虛浮的。」

"Charm is deceptive, and beauty is fleeting."

(箴言 Proverbs 31:30)

【花樣人間 II】
鬢旁花、足下花，
誰艷誰殘一步差，
哪知命數不上下，
誰也不比誰高雅。

Flowery World III

Flowers at the bosom,
flowers on the grave.
With the cheer,
for the mourning,
who sees through the way?
Who's not a sand
in the wind of fate?
Who allows blessings
or curses
in whose home to stay?

歡慶的時刻、哀傷的時刻，往往都是能看見花的時刻。

到底是誰發明花的呢？

Moments of celebration, and moments of sadness,

are often moments when you can see flowers.

Who invented flowers?

「野地裏的草今天還在,明天就丟在爐裏, 神還給他這樣的妝飾,何況你們呢?」

" If that is how God clothes the grass of the field, which is here today and tomorrow is thrown into the fire, will he not much more clothe you?"

(馬太福音 Matthew 6:30)

【花樣人間 III】
懷裏花、墓前花,
誰悲誰喜誰看化?
哪人不是風中沙?
誰定禍福落誰家?

Flowery World IV

Flowers as talk,
flowers as plants.
Who takes time
to see which ones stand?
Who's not busy
racing in the trend?
Who would slow down,
and cast a flower
just a glance?

大自然總是能令人心神寧定，也許是因為大自然的東西沒有虛假。

Nature can always calm your mind,

perhaps the reason is that there is nothing fake in nature.

「*你們要休息，要知道我是 神！*」

"*Be still, and know that I am God!*"

（詩篇 Psalm 46:10）

【花樣人間 IV】

墜天花，種鮮花，
誰鑑時日辨真假？
哪位不在競走馬？
誰願緩步細看花？

【花非花】

葉非葉、花非花，
粉紅嫩綠滙一把，
蔚藍映襯嬌可嘉，
何名何稱何足掛？
花乘葉、葉承花，
美態怡人目不暇，
無耐歲月盜芳華，
賞之莫待花非花。

珍惜今天的美好，別為明天積存無謂的惋惜。

Cherish the beauty of today,

and don't store up unnecessary regrets for tomorrow.

「天地都要過去。」

"Heaven and earth will pass away."

（馬可福音 新譯本 Mark 13:31）

Flowers, not Flowers

Leaves are not leaves,
flowers are not flowers.
But pink and green
so delicately splattered.
Bright blue in support
and make them tenderer.
What's the title?
What it is called?
Does it matter?
Flowers on leaves,
leaves hold flowers.
How delightful it is
for my eyes to bear!
Months and years
will surely steal them, however.
Behold!
Don't wait until
when leaves are not leaves,
and flowers are not flowers.

The Tree

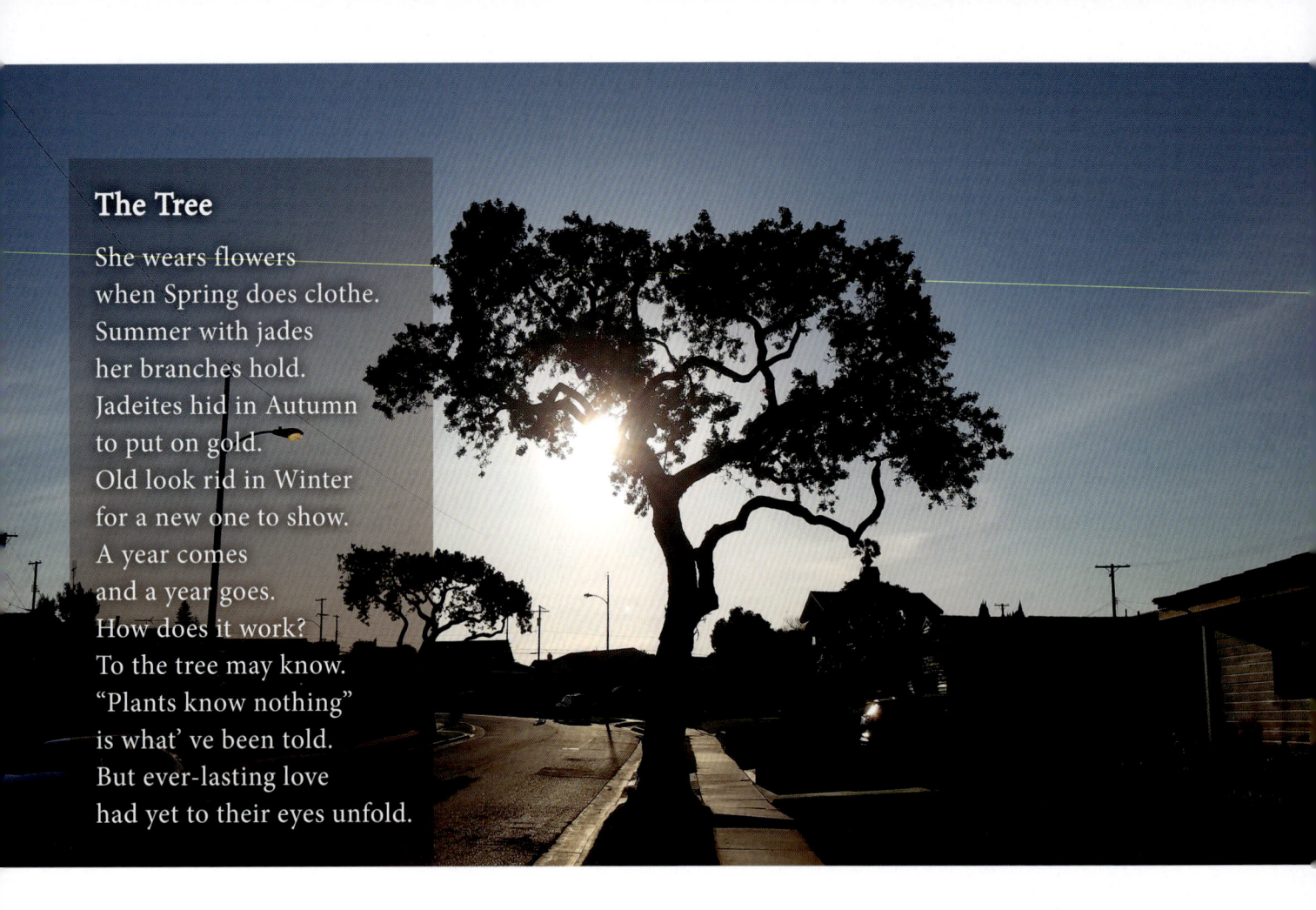

She wears flowers
when Spring does clothe.
Summer with jades
her branches hold.
Jadeites hid in Autumn
to put on gold.
Old look rid in Winter
for a new one to show.
A year comes
and a year goes.
How does it work?
To the tree may know.
"Plants know nothing"
is what've been told.
But ever-lasting love
had yet to their eyes unfold.

這樹也好，那樹也好，不是都在
春、夏、秋、冬的週而復始裏守護著大地嗎？

Whether it is this tree or that tree, aren't they all guarding the earth
throughout the cycle of spring, summer, autumn, and winter?

「祂不叫你的腳搖動;保護你的必不打盹!」

"He will not let your foot slip—
　　He who watches over you will not slumber."

(詩篇 Psalm 121:3)

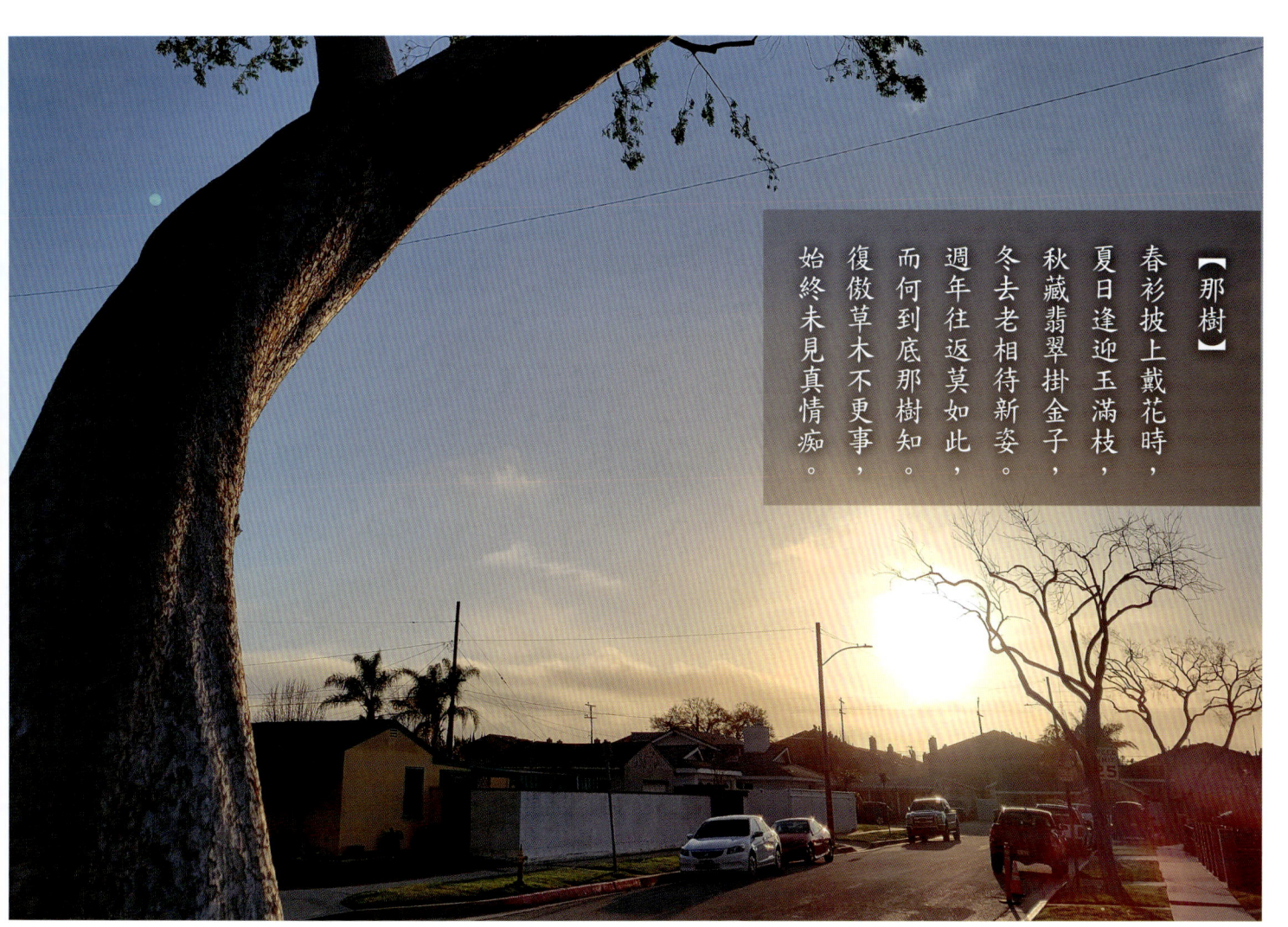

【那樹】

春衫披上戴花時,
夏日逢迎玉滿枝,
秋藏翡翠掛金子,
冬去老相待新姿。
週年往返莫如此,
而何到底那樹知,
復傲草木不更事,
始終未見真情痴。

※ 秋藏翡翠掛金子:秋天的葉子由翠綠變成金黃。

Violet Makeup

Jacaranda blushing in her blue.
The violet makeup is put on for whom?
Once near hopeless,
she yearned for someone's woo.
Now favourably bathing
in the spring wind blew.

不住尋求、不住禱告，總有一天你會得到的。

Keep on seeking, keep on praying,
and one day you shall receive.

「我（耶穌）實實在在地告訴你們，你們奉我的名無論向父（神）求甚麼，祂會賜給你們。」

"Very truly I(Jesus) tell you, my Father will give you whatever you ask in my name."

(約翰福音 John 16:23)

【紫妝】

楹藍非藍略提紅，
紫妝嬌顏為誰用？
曾經臨絕盼情濃，
今得青睞沐春風。

※ 楹藍：指藍花楹，其花語為「在絕望中等待愛情」。

Befriend Wind and Flowers

Wind, my companion.
Flowers, my friends.
Cool down summer,
and bring pleasant scents.

Flowers must dwindle.
Wind can't be retained.
Gone and return
and their company remains.

Wind,
cold but not that cold
to speak insult.
Flowers,
fall yet never fall
into resentment as a result.

Along the ensemble
of dogs and birds at times,
a moment of solitude
restores me peace of mind.

【友風花】

風為朋，花為友，
炎夏送涼傳清幽，
花易瘦，風難留，
去亦復還伴左右。
風冷未曾冷語羞，
花落從不落怨仇，
偶有鳥鳴犬吠湊，
暫避人言心安悠。

人言其實可以好像夏天的風和春天的花的。

In fact, human words can be like
the wind in summer and flowers in spring.

「懷抱有時，不抱有時。」

"A time to embrace
and a time to refrain from embracing."

(傳道書 Ecclesiastes 3:5)

鼓勵說：「繼續努力！」

批判說：「你哪裏有問題了？」

把它們當作衣服般，先往自己試試喜歡的一款吧！

Encouragement says, "Keep up the good work!"

Criticism says, "What's wrong with you?"

Treat them as clothes, try the one that you like on!

「一句話說得合宜，就如金蘋果在銀網子裏。」

"A word fitly spoken is like apples of gold in a setting of silver."

（箴言 Proverbs ESV 25:11）

【人言可貴】
人之交臂何以牽？
言而有信立底線，
可畏虛表流膚淺，
貴在摯誠互勵勉。

Precious Words

A person with another,
what makes
their friendship abide?
Keeping one's word
marks the bottom line.
Dreadful is pretending,
to shallowness it drives.
Encouragement in sincerity
is always valued high.

與其惋惜今天的失落，何不期待發現明天的美好？

Instead of pitying the downs of today, why not look forward to discovering the beauty of tomorrow?

「祂的恩典乃是一生之久。一宿雖然有哭泣，早晨便必歡呼。」
"His favour lasts a lifetime; weeping may stay for the night, but rejoicing comes in the morning."

(詩篇 Psalm 30:5)

Sweeter than Yesterday

From dawn to dusk,
to when the night is laid,
flowers still scent
yet some are drifting away.
Tomorrow will come
with the same scene to play,
But looking forward to
the scent of flowers
will be sweeter than yesterday.

【花勝昨】
東昇西沉夜幕落，
芬芳未息花漂泊。
明日復來復輪廓，
且待花香猶勝昨。

Slow the Fading Down

At the dressing table,
sighed lightly.
Who can save my withering beauty?
On the years I blame,
so greedy.
Take up my days relentlessly.

How many dreams were shattered?
How often passion did falter?
How many a time unflustered?
How often laughters cover tears?

You worry,
yet "worry" doesn't worry you!
In your chest,
to your health,
it brutely rules.
On your forehead,
amid your brows,
it carves so cruel.
Beauty fades,
and more quickly will it do.

No match is youth for worry.
Let not worry
roll in your bosom so wildly.
Remember of old,
the Lord hushed the sea of stormy.
Regain in deep
your calm and serenity.

焦慮這回事比起要焦慮的事情更可怕。

The matter of anxiety is more dreadful than the things to be anxious about.

「你們中間誰能用憂慮使自己的壽命延長一刻呢？」

"Who of you by worrying can add a single hour to your life?"

（路加福音 新譯本 Luke 12:25）

【緩色退】

倚粧台，輕嗟嘆，
恨裏不懂恨愁煩，
老掉朱顏誰可挽？
藏堵胸懷敗肝膽，
怨年日，不勝貪，
眉間額上刻兩彎，
奪過歲月不歸還。
漸暗花容添衰殘。
幾回夢碎成空盼？
韶華莫敵愁來犯，
幾番意興漸闌珊？
別任愁緒懷裡翻。
幾許自己處平淡？
復思神子靜波瀾，
幾多笑臉掩淚彈？
心安釋然復舒坦。

Peace

Day in, day out,
striving in the wind.
Earned all praises
with the hard works seen.
Works have no end
but end up in emptiness.
"Life has an end"
stands on its truthfulness.
Shackles are on
when toiling all days.
A life for but works,
what a heavy price to pay!
Why not enjoy
the true wealth you have?
And let not peace be
held up in heaven instead.

內心沒有平安，會否是太多的籌算堵塞了心房？

Without peace of mind, would it be too many plans clogged up the heart?

【平安】

朝朝暮暮營風下，
劬勞一生眾所誇，
事無盡頭實虛空，
壽有終時未作假。
汲汲渡日自披枷，
償願以命是何價？
且享既得真資財，
別把平安擱天家。

「得力在乎平靜安穩。」
"In quietness and trust is your strength."
(以賽亞書 Isaiah 30:15)

※ 汲汲：指「急忙地」。

時間和身心健康才是生命最大的資源，
而金錢只不過是用這些資源交換得來的工具罷了。

Time, and physical and mental health are the greatest resources in life,
while money is but a tool exchanged by using these resources.

「人若賺得全世界，卻賠上自己的生命，有甚麼好處呢？
人還能用甚麼換回自己的生命呢？」

"What good will it be for someone to gain the whole world, yet forfeit their soul?
Or what can anyone give in exchange for their soul?"

（馬太福音 新譯本 Matthew 16:26）

【未通神】
人留財帛天留人，
富可敵國未通神，
一朝魄散獨留身，
萬金難押半縷魂。

Can't Trade with God

People keep money,
God keeps people.
Not to the richest
does God's will be sold.
Once a spirit is taken,
the body is left, though.
No wealth is fair
to pledge even half a soul.

Gather the Warmth

Daytime lapsing
while dusk comes close.
Time to return
as weary do the flowers show.
Humbly the sun recedes
to welcome the night as host.
Gather the warmth remains
for a good night's sleep to hold.

【朝花夕拾】
朝時已遠暮漸近，
花呈倦容表歸心，
夕陽謙退迎夜臨，
拾起餘溫暖安寢。

休息是一回事，安然地休息又是另一回事。

Resting is one thing, resting peacefully is another.

「惟有 神所親愛的，必叫他安然睡覺。」

"He(God) grants sleep to those he loves."

(詩篇 Psalm 127:2)

【風雨復晴】
風侵江河漣紋生，
雨襲湖泊璃塵滾，
復見動盪非永恆，
晴空終現照來晨。

※ 璃塵滾：揚起的玻璃粉塵，比喻暴雨擊在湖面所濺起的綿密水花。

終會有天青。

There will finally be a blue sky.

「就是蝗蟲、蝻子、螞蚱、剪蟲，那些年（牠們）所吃的，我（神）要補還你們。」

"I(God) will repay you for the years the locusts have eaten—
the great locust and the young locust,
the other locusts and the locust swarm."

（約珥書 Joel 2:25）

A Clear Sky Restored

Wind strikes rivers
spurs ripples grow.
Rain pounds the lake
makes stardust roll.
Seeing again that
turmoil is not eternal.
Clear sky must come
in a better tomorrow.

Born Again

Among the bushes,
it dances gracefully.
In the Wind,
it travels deftly.
On a leaf, it rests briefly.
To flowers,
its bearing beats rivalry.

Thought who,
when it was little enough,
but a worm
crawled along the filthy mud?
In an ugly cocoon was it locked up,
dull as the scab,
seemed death had already struck.

Until the time was fulfilled,
wings were grown
with elegance to thrill.
And in a moment still,
flutters to prove its form of new.

Butterfly,
in the human world it passes by.
Phoenix,
in the open sky it overrides.
Both born again
when comparing them side by side,
Couldn't we connect them
with a family line?

【重生】

叢中翩翩舞,
風裏展瀟灑,
葉上稍安歇,
姿態猶勝花。
誰思時還幼,
作蟲泥上爬,
更囚陋蛹中,
息薄死如痂。
且待時日滿,
添翼添優雅;
再待須臾往,
振翅證轉化。
粉蝶人間過,
鳳凰凌大遐,
重生相比擬,
莫非是一家?

※ 凌大遐:凌,登上;大遐,高遠的上空。

固有的心態往往是帶來束縛的陋蛹,掙脫了方能振翅飛翔。

An inherent mindset is often a cocoon that brings constraints.
Only when you break free can you fly.

「不要效法這個世界,只要心意更新而變化。」
"Do not conform to the pattern of this world, but
be transformed by the renewing of your mind."

(羅馬書 Romans 12:2)

【一天】

蔚藍天，闊無邊，
延綿舖張蓋萬千。
風雲常變晴終現，
孜孜普照歲連連。
暮時天，素顏斂，
滿臉嫣然華容艷，
紅霞片片抹作胭，
醉態醉人君莫羨。
入夜天，一身靛，
深邃沉靜掛垂簾。
月微還伴星點點，
暗燈呼君入安眠。
另一天，透光線，
朝暉四射若加冕；
昨日晦暗留以前，
佩戴輝煌自今天。

重新出發，活在當下。

Start over and live in the present.

One sky, One day

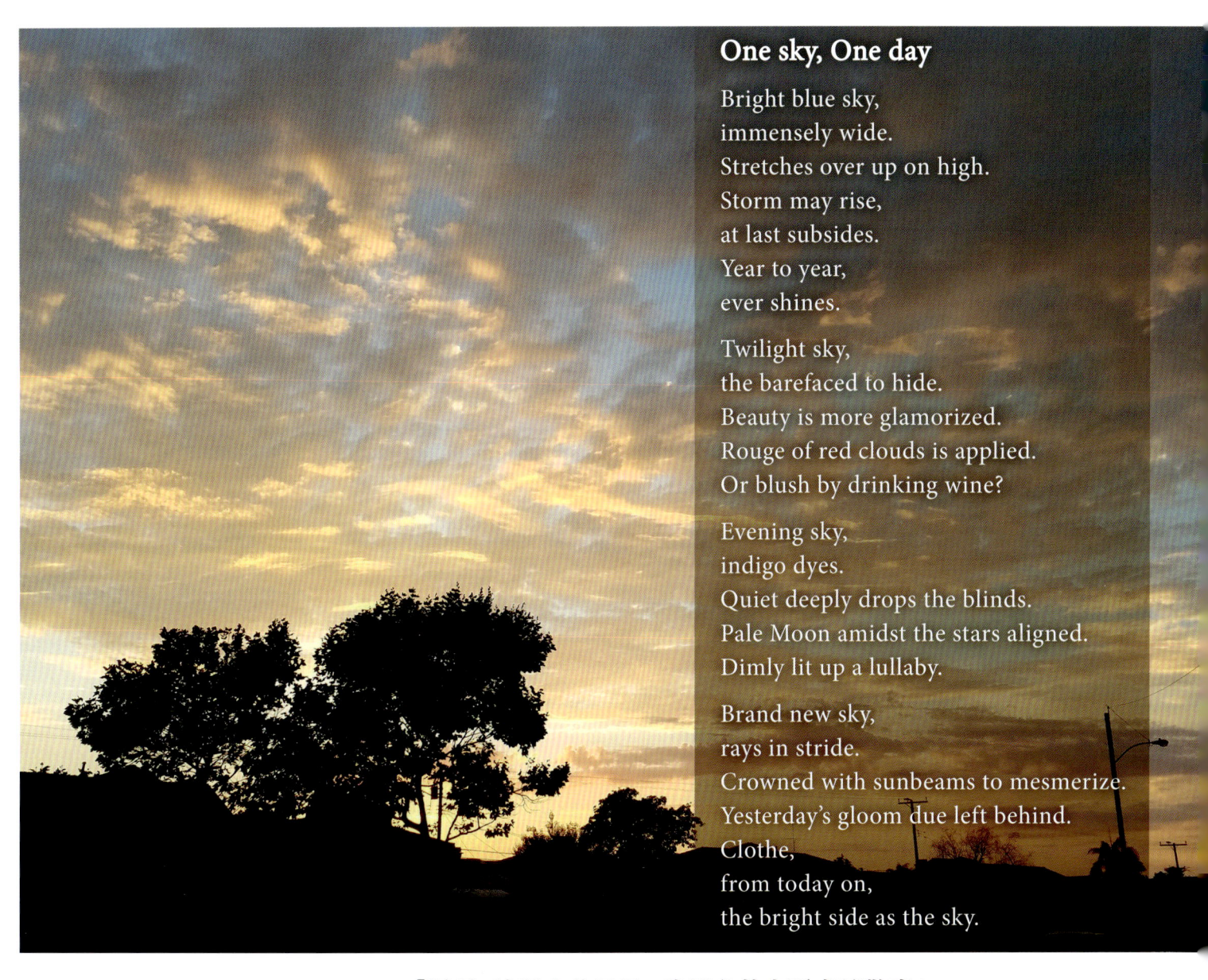

Bright blue sky,
immensely wide.
Stretches over up on high.
Storm may rise,
at last subsides.
Year to year,
ever shines.

Twilight sky,
the barefaced to hide.
Beauty is more glamorized.
Rouge of red clouds is applied.
Or blush by drinking wine?

Evening sky,
indigo dyes.
Quiet deeply drops the blinds.
Pale Moon amidst the stars aligned.
Dimly lit up a lullaby.

Brand new sky,
rays in stride.
Crowned with sunbeams to mesmerize.
Yesterday's gloom due left behind.
Clothe,
from today on,
the bright side as the sky.

「這是 神所定的日子，我們在其中要高興歡喜！」

"The Lord has done it this very day; let us rejoice today and be glad."

(詩篇 Psalm 118:24)

謝詞

　　古詩體的寫作對我來說一直是一件神蹟奇事。起初就像開展了一門奢華的新嗜好，我只能負擔得起偶爾才做出點東西來，而每當一首新作寫成，我都會欣喜若狂並滿懷感激，但在那時我遠遠還沒有看到這回事有多麼的神奇。直到我的作品數量可以用雙位數字來統計：20、50、接著是100，然後慢慢的超過150，並且它們寫成的時期，正值我為着能專注於學習本地語言來紮根移民而在避免閱讀中文書籍；然而在閱讀英文書籍方面卻因着在大學進修，而成為必要。再進一步回顧我的年少日子：一個不曾用功的學生，愛買、愛藏卻不愛讀書的書蟲；於是妨礙我寫作中文詩的阻力建立起來了，讓整件事變得就像神蹟般。也許只有我的國語能力給我在寫作上稍添了一點條理吧！那麼一點的助力面對諸多的阻力，符合上帝在尋求祂的人身上工作的模式，我怎能不將榮耀歸給神呢？

　　透過詩作向那些心靈軟弱和疲乏的人伸出援手是我的職份。我太太讓我感到蒙福，因為她的看法與我一致。她把這本詩集的製作視為我的工作而不是額外的事情。有時候我的信心也會因着主流的規章而動搖：定時上班和定期支薪；只是她會指出我們的充足，好叫我能保持冷靜並繼續前行。她在我腦海裏平靜了一個小風暴，這是她經常施行的微型神蹟。她也是我的啦啦隊長：讚嘆與點頭總是她在看到書中內容所給出的反應。還有比這樣更大的支持麼？謝謝妳！我親愛的妻子，妳是最優秀的！

　　文字、空白和圖片，所有這些視覺元素都必須按一定的規律舖陳，才能與讀者有效溝通，換言之——平面設計之事也。我擁有這些足叫我能完成這事的觸覺和技能，要歸功於兩位男士，談振邦先生和梅智斌先生。談振邦先生推薦我加入梅智斌先生的多媒體製作團隊，是在九十年代末，當時全球網路產業蓬勃發展，而我就迫切需要一份工作；打從那時起，我在香港從事該行業的三分之二時間裏，梅智斌先生一直予以照顧。兩位男士都是思維敏捷，才華洋溢，對朋友也很直率。談振邦先生是一位非常有能力的網頁設計師，他向新手的我「加載」了他實用的網頁設計技巧，讓我能輕鬆啟航。而作為老闆的梅智斌先生極盡坦誠，對我早期作品的批判從不遮掩，也對我後期作品的認可和讚揚毫不吝嗇。謝謝你們，芒果和 Benny，感謝你們對我的接納和友誼，也感謝你們為我的專業成長作出了扶持。

黃永輝教士、劉西傳道和劉王邦聰師母，這些守望我和淑蘭靈命成長的屬靈父母，感謝您們多年來的禱告支持，也非常感激您們花時間閱讀這本書，並執筆撰序以使其更加完整，更不消說當中的鼓勵了。

　　生活是艱苦的，當得着靈感寫詩的一剎那，就像室內的空氣將盡，卻發現有一扇可以打開的窗。透過這扇窗，我可以呼吸新鮮空氣，振作精神，我也可以仰望天空，稱奇於之上的天體序列，驚嘆於其下的地上受造。生活是十分艱苦的，彷彿雨下連連，但即便如此，我還是會打開窗，呼吸、仰望，更慶賀那生機勃勃的綠草和熱情洋溢的紅葉在雨中閃閃發光，因為它們就是你們的支持的體現，是我力量復興背後叫我堅毅往前的聲聲喝采。

　　謝謝你們！我親愛的朋友們！

Acknowledgements

Writing ancient-style Chinese poetry has always been a miraculous work to me. Initially, it was like starting a new luxurious hobby where I could only afford to work something out occasionally. I was ecstatic and grateful whenever I wrote a new poem. Yet back then, far be it from me to see the matter as miraculous. Until the number of my works could be counted in double digits: 20, 50, then 100, and eventually over 150, where they were written in a period when I refrained from reading Chinese books for me to focus on picking up the local language to root my immigration. In the meantime, reading English books, however, was a must due to college. Looking further back at my youth history, I was a rather lazy student and a bookworm who cared about buying and collecting books instead of reading them. Odds were built against my Chinese poetry writing and making the business miraculous. Only my Mandarin language skills may give me a little more structure in my writing. A bit of favour but plenty of odds; it fits how God works in those seeking Him. How could I not ascribe the glory to God?

Reaching out to those who may be fainthearted and weary in soul through poetry is my call of duty. Blessed is me for my wife, Helen, who is on the same page as me. She views my making of this book as my job instead of doing something extra. Sometimes, my faith wavers when I look at the majority norm: you go to work at a set time and bring home an income on a set day. Yet she would point out our sufficiency for me to keep calm and rock on. She calmed the little storm in my mind, a subtle miracle she always performs. She is also the cheerleader for this project. Praising and nodding are always her responses when viewing the content. Could there be more significant support than that? Thank You, my dear wife, Helen! You are the best!

    The texts, the blank, and the pictures, all these visual elements have to be laid out in a particular order to effectively communicate with the readers, in a nutshell, graphic design. My senses and skills are good enough to get the job done, and two gentlemen due the credits, Mr. Mango Tam and Mr. Benny Mui. Mango referred me to be a member of Benny's multimedia production team back at the very end of the 90s when the worldwide web industry was soaring, and I direly needed a job. From then on, Benny has been watching over me for two-thirds of my servicing time in the industry. The two gentlemen are both quick-witted, talented, and sincere to friends. Mango, a very competent web designer, loaded me with his practical web design tricks for my easy start-up when I was a newbie. While Benny, the boss, as honest as one can be, didn't conceal his criticism of my early works and never withheld his recognition and praise on my latter productions. Thank you, Mango and Benny, my dear brothers, for your acceptance and friendship of all times, and thank you for scaffolding me in my professional growth.

Samuel Wong, Charles Liu, and Joyce Liu are the spiritual parents of Helen and me, who watch over our growth in faith. Thank you for your prayers of support throughout the years. I greatly appreciate your time reading this book and giving your forewords to make it more complete, not to mention the encouragement within.

Life is tough. When it comes to the moment of inspiration to write a poem, it is like air is running out in the room, but a window can be opened is found. Through this window, I can breathe fresh air and spirit up, see the sky, wonder at the alignment of the celestial bodies above, and be amazed at the earthly creation below. Life is so tough, as if it is always raining. But even so, I will open the window to breathe, to see, and to celebrate the vibrant meadow and the zesty red leaves both gleaming in the rain, as they are the embodiment of your support, the cheer for me to hang on in a resurgence of strength.

Thank You! All my dear friends!

國家圖書館出版品預行編目(CIP)資料

有時 = A time / 徐仰聖(Frank Chui)作. -- 初版. --
臺北市：華品文創出版股份有限公司, 2025.03
　　面；　公分
中英對照
ISBN 978-626-7614-07-5(精裝)

1.CST: 聖詩

244.4　　　　　　　　　　　　114002839